Here's how to use this coloring book:

Choose Your Space: Find a comfy spot with your coloring supplies handy.

Intention Setting: Think of your goals and what you want to manifest.

Pick a Page: Open the book and select a mandala page that resonates.

Color with Intent: As you color, imagine each stroke bringing your intentions to life.

Connect with Quotes: Read the quotes and let them sink in as you color.

Express Gratitude: Write down, every day, the things you are grateful for.

Visualize Success: Imagine your dreams as reality while coloring, seeing your vision board and exercising.

Repeat the Process: Color more pages to reinforce your focus on your goals.

Stay Present: Enjoy the mindful act of coloring and being in the moment.

Make it Routine: Dedicate regular time to coloring and manifesting.

Enjoy and Believe: Embrace the joy of coloring and believe in your dreams.

With each stroke, exercise, and visualization, you're taking steps to attract your dream life.

Let's explore the core principles of manifestation mastery!

Deep Belief: Manifestation hinges on your unwavering belief. Your thoughts and intentions are energetic vibrations that interact with the cosmos. True manifestation isn't just surface positivity but an ingrained conviction that aligns your subconscious with your conscious desires.

Aligning Vibrations: Each thought carries a unique energy frequency. Like musical notes, similar energies attract. Picture your intentions as vibrational threads connecting you to your desires, creating an energetic symphony.

Quantum Connection: Quantum physics reveals the interconnectedness of all things. Your thoughts ripple through this cosmic network, touching everything. View each coloring session as meditation, amplifying your intentions and tapping into universal energy.
Patience and Persistence: Manifestation is a journey, not a sprint. Think of it as tending a garden; the universe responds to dedication. Time and persistence are allies as you contribute to your manifestation tapestry.

Inspired Action: Aligned actions bridge the ethereal and physical. Each color stroke represents intention and progress. Contemplate actions that align with your manifestations; the universe meets you halfway.

Consider each page in this guide as a canvas for your manifestation journey. The spaces you fill with color are energetic portals, connecting your consciousness to the universe's energy. Let coloring be your meditation, harmonizing your intentions with cosmic energies.

May your journey be one of resonance and connection, where your thoughts and intentions weave into the universe's fabric. Embrace the enchantment of manifesting, for every thought, intention, and color shapes your reality.

Paint your life with abundance!

You radiate abundance in all directions!

Trust your inner guidance to manifest your desires!

I am grateful for:
My manifestation:
VISION BOARD

Use colors that represent success and prosperity.

Imagine these qualities being drawn to you.

Be a magnet for prosperity and success!

I am grateful for:

My manifestation:

VISION BOARD

As you color the mandala, feel the flow of abundance
surrounding you, like a gentle stream.

Abundance flows effortlessly into your life.

I am grateful for:

My manifestation:

VISION BOARD

As you color, imagine your mandala as a cosmic scene,
reflecting the vastness of universal abundance.

Embrace
the universe's gifts!

I am grateful for:
My manifestation:
VISION BOARD

Paint your life with abundance!

I am grateful for:

My manifestation:

VISION BOARD

As you color, visualize your mandala as a birth
certificate, declaring your birthright to abundance.
Abundance is your
birthright, claim it!

I am grateful for:

My manifestation:

VISION BOARD

Use vibrant colors in your mandala, attracting
prosperity symbols.
Attract prosperity like
a magnet attracts iron!

I am grateful for:
My manifestation:
VISION BOARD

The image represent yourself as a channel, with abundance flowing through you. Color it with energy.

Be a conduit for the universe's abundance!

I am grateful for:
My manifestation:
VISION BOARD

Use harmonious colors when you coloring.
The universe conspires
in your favor!

I am grateful for:
My manifestation:
VISION BOARD

Color the image confidently and know abundance
is your natural state of mind.
Abundance is your
natural state of being!

I am grateful for:

My manifestation:

VISION BOARD

Color the flowers as it blooms with abundance.
Your thoughts are
seeds of abundance!

I am grateful for:

My manifestation:

As you color, feel the overflowing of abundance in your heart.
Color it to represent giving and receiving.

You are abundance,
giving and receiving.

I am grateful for:

My manifestation:

VISION BOARD

Abundance is your birthright, claim it!

I am grateful for:

My manifestation:

VISION BOARD

Fill in the mandala with colors that evoke feelings
of joy and gratitude, infusing it with positive energy.

Abundance flows
effortlessly into your life!

I am grateful for:

My manifestation:

VISION BOARD

Use warm, vibrant colors to represent the abundance of love in your life. Feel the warmth as you color.
Abundance flows within and around you!

I am grateful for:

My manifestation:

VISION BOARD

Choose colors that symbolize wealth and prosperity.
As you color, imagine these qualities filling your life.
You are a magnet for prosperity and success!

I am grateful for:
My manifestation:
VISION BOARD

Focus on grounding colors like earthy browns and greens
to bring stability and abundance to your mandala.

Abundance is your natural state of being!

I am grateful for:

My manifestation:

VISION BOARD

Select calming, cool colors to represent the abundance
of peace in your life. Feel a sense of calm as you color.

You are in alignment with
the flow of abundance!

I am grateful for:

My manifestation:

Fill the mandala with shades of blue, symbolizing the
abundance of creativity and self-expression within you.
Your thoughts are
seeds of abundance!

I am grateful for:

My manifestation:

VISION BOARD

Use shades of gold and yellow to represent the abundance
of wisdom. Feel yourself growing wiser as you color.

You radiate abundance
in all directions!

I am grateful for:
My manifestation:
VISION BOARD

Fill your mandala with colors associated with adventure and exploration. Imagine new experiences awaiting you.

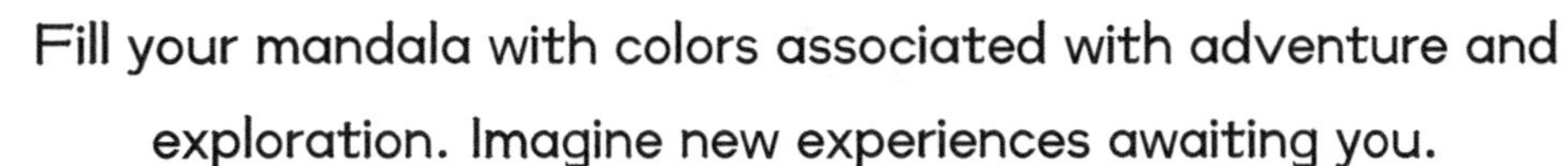

Every day is a treasure trove of opportunities!

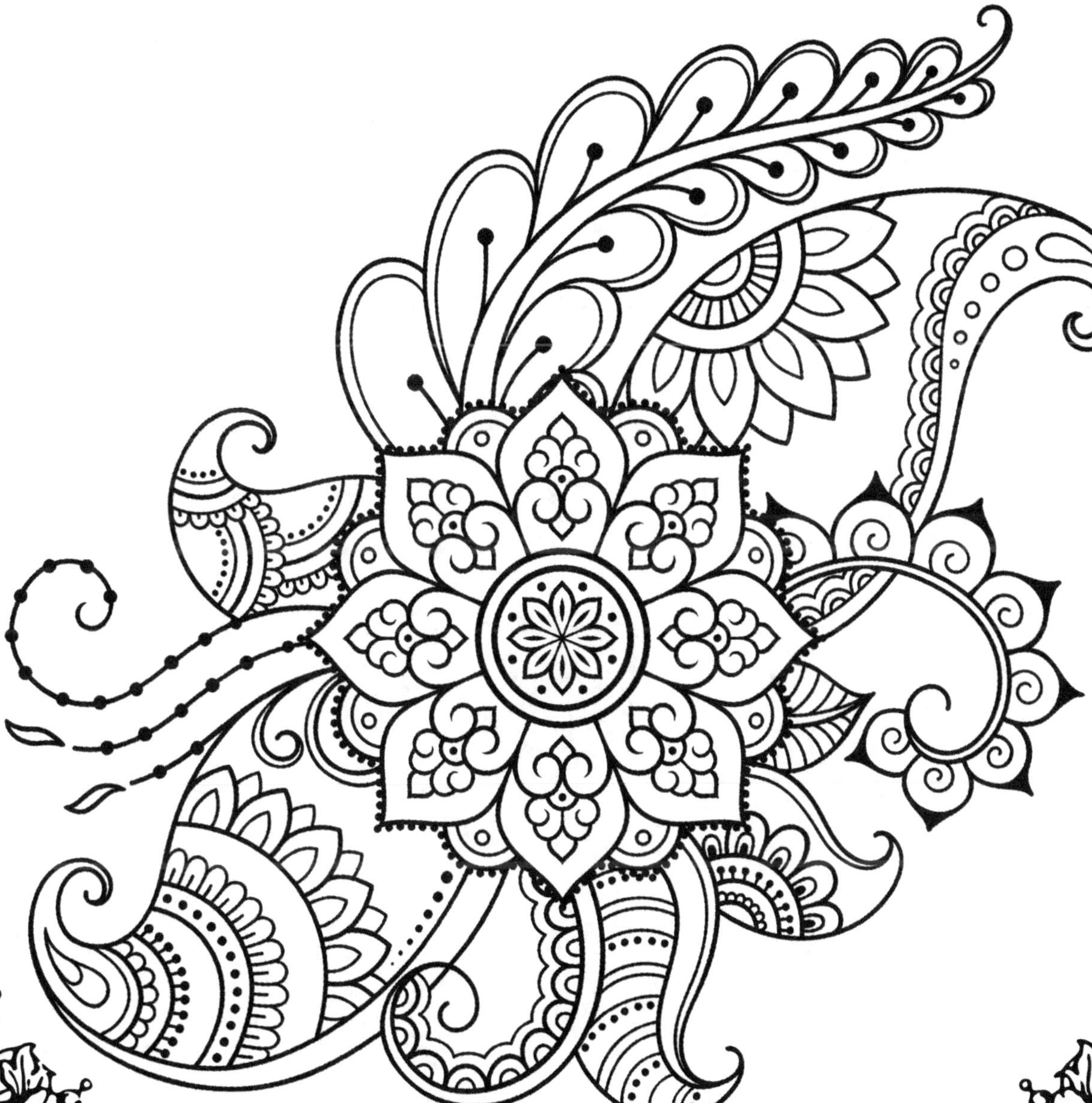

I am grateful for:

My manifestation:

VISION BOARD

Use a variety of shades to depict the diverse abundance
in your life, from material wealth to emotional richness.

Abundance is a frequency you tune into!

I am grateful for:

My manifestation:

VISION BOARD

As you color, repeat the affirmation "I am worthy"
and feel your sense of self-worth growing.
You are worthy of
life's abundant gifts!

I am grateful for:

My manifestation:

VISION BOARD

Focus on pastel colors to represent the gentleness and abundance of kindness in your interactions.

Your mindset reflects your abundance!

I am grateful for:

My manifestation:

VISION BOARD

Select vibrant colors to symbolize the passion and enthusiasm that abundance can bring. Feel the energy as you color.

Abundance expands
with gratitude!

I am grateful for:

My manifestation:

VISION BOARD

Use shades of purple to represent the spiritual abundance in your life. Visualize a deep sense of connection as you color.

The more you celebrate, the more there is to celebrate!

I am grateful for:

My manifestation:

VISION BOARD

Fill with colors that remind you of the
beauty and abundance of nature.
Feel connected to the natural world as you color.
Prosperity is the
consciousness to create!

I am grateful for:

My manifestation:

VISION BOARD

Choose colors that reflect the abundance of time and freedom in your life. Feel the relaxation and freedom as you color.
Be open to all the universe's abundance!

I am grateful for:
My manifestation:
VISION BOARD

Focus on metallic colors like silver and bronze to symbolize the abundance of achievement and recognition in your life.

Abundance is not limited; it is infinite.

I am grateful for:

My manifestation:

VISION BOARD

Use colors that represent the inner abundance within you, and fill the mandala with them.

Abundance flows from within!

I am grateful for:

My manifestation:

VISION BOARD

Fill your mandala with shades of orange to depict the
abundance of creativity and passion.
Feel your creative energy flowing.

Abundance flows
where intention goes!

I am grateful for:
My manifestation:
VISION BOARD

Select colors that represent the abundance of positive
relationships and connections in your life.
Feel the love and support as you color.
Be open for all the
universe's blessings.

I am grateful for:

My manifestation:

VISION BOARD

As you color, imagine yourself drawing in the experiences you want to manifest.

You are a magnet for the experiences you desire!

I am grateful for:
My manifestation:
VISION BOARD

Use colors that resonate with high energy, like bright yellows and oranges. As you color, visualize the energetic vibrations of your desires.

Feel the vibrations of your desires!

I am grateful for:
My manifestation:
VISION BOARD

Use colors that represents your five senses (sight, sound, touch, taste, and smell). As you color each sense, think about how they align with your manifestations.

Your senses align
with your manifestations!

I am grateful for:

My manifestation:

Color the mandala with colors that represent opportunities, such as green and gold. Focus on feeling the opportunities opening up in your life as you color.

Sense the opportunities unfolding for you!

I am grateful for:
My manifestation:
VISION BOARD

Choose colors by using colors that represent different emotions. As you color each section, connect with the emotions that guide you towards your dreams.

Your emotions guide you towards your dreams!

I am grateful for:

My manifestation:

VISION BOARD

As you color, visualize yourself walking a path to success,
trusting your inner guidance to lead you to your desires.
Trust your inner guidance
to manifest your desires!

I am grateful for:
My manifestation:
VISION BOARD

Color the mandala using colors that for you, represent the flow of abundance. Focus on sensing this universal abundance as you color.

Feel the universe's abundance within you!

I am grateful for:

My manifestation:

VISION BOARD

Color the mandala with colors that make you feel successful.

Embrace the sensations of success as you color.

Embrace success and achievement!

I am grateful for:

My manifestation:

VISION BOARD

As you color the mandala, think about how you are attuned
to the signs of your manifestations coming to fruition.
Be attuned to the
signs of the manifestations!

I am grateful for:

My manifestation:

VISION BOARD

Color with grounding colors that represent the present moment. As you color, focus on feeling the presence of your desires in the present.

Feel the presence of your desires in the now!

I am grateful for:

My manifestation:

VISION BOARD

Color with warm, inviting colors that represent the flow of love. Imagine love easily entering your life as you color.

Thoughts, beliefs, and actions create wealth and success!

I am grateful for:
My manifestation:
VISION BOARD

While coloring, visualize your financial goals and use green
and gold to highlight areas that represent money and success."

Your mind is the key to
manifest money and success.

I am grateful for:

My manifestation:

VISION BOARD

While coloring, focus on your vision of success and choose shades of blue and purple to emphasize clarity and creativity.

Believe in yourself, attract wealth and success!

I am grateful for:

My manifestation:

VISION BOARD

As you color, be mindful of cultivating an abundance mindset.
Add green and blue to promote balance and trust within the design.
Success flows when aligned with purpose!

I am grateful for:

My manifestation:

VISION BOARD

Color the mandala and feel yourself worthy of deep
and meaningful connections.

You deserve meaningful
connections!

I am grateful for:

My manifestation:

VISION BOARD

Imagine the mandala representing your dream career.
Incorporate blue and goldy yellow into the existing elements to inspire success.
Clear vision and self-belief manifest abundance!

I am grateful for:

My manifestation:

VISION BOARD

As you color, visualize yourself surrounded by
loving souls who resonate with your path.

Attract souls who align with your journey!

I am grateful for:

My manifestation:

Bring awareness to the richness already present in your life. Use green and yellow to amplify the feeling of abundance within the design.
Abundance is a state you can manifest!

I am grateful for:
My manifestation:
VISION BOARD

Meditate on financial goals while coloring.

Your mind is the key to manifest money and success!

I am grateful for:

My manifestation:

VISION BOARD

Practice gratitude while coloring.
Persistence and belief lead to success!

I am grateful for:

My manifestation:

VISION BOARD

Color the mandala with bright, invigorating colors that
represent vibrant health. As you color, imagine health flowing
into your life effortlessly.

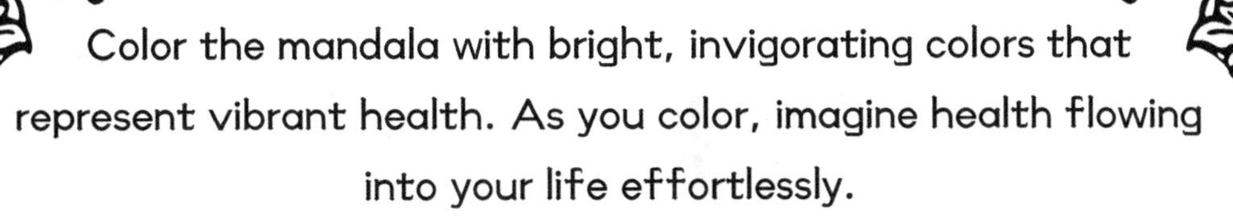

Vibrant health flows effortlessly into your life!

I am grateful for:

My manifestation:

VISION BOARD

Use colors that resonate with attraction. As you color, envision yourself attracting optimal well-being and health.

You are a magnet for optimal well-being!

I am grateful for:
My manifestation:
VISION BOARD

Feel and imagine your body as a temple
of health as you color.
Your body is a temple
of health and vitality!

I am grateful for:

My manifestation:

VISION BOARD

As you color, focus on trusting your body's innate wisdom and its ability to heal.

Mindset shapes your reality, focus on abundance!

I am grateful for:
My manifestation:
VISION BOARD

As you color, feel yourself worthy of good health and well-being.

You are deserving of good health and well-being!

I am grateful for:

My manifestation:

VISION BOARD

As you color, focus on feeling a healthy lifestyle in the here and now.

Embrace a healthy life in the present moment!

I am grateful for:
My manifestation:
VISION BOARD

As you color, imagine wellness effortlessly
entering your life.

Attract wellness
into your life with ease!

I am grateful for:

My manifestation:

VISION BOARD

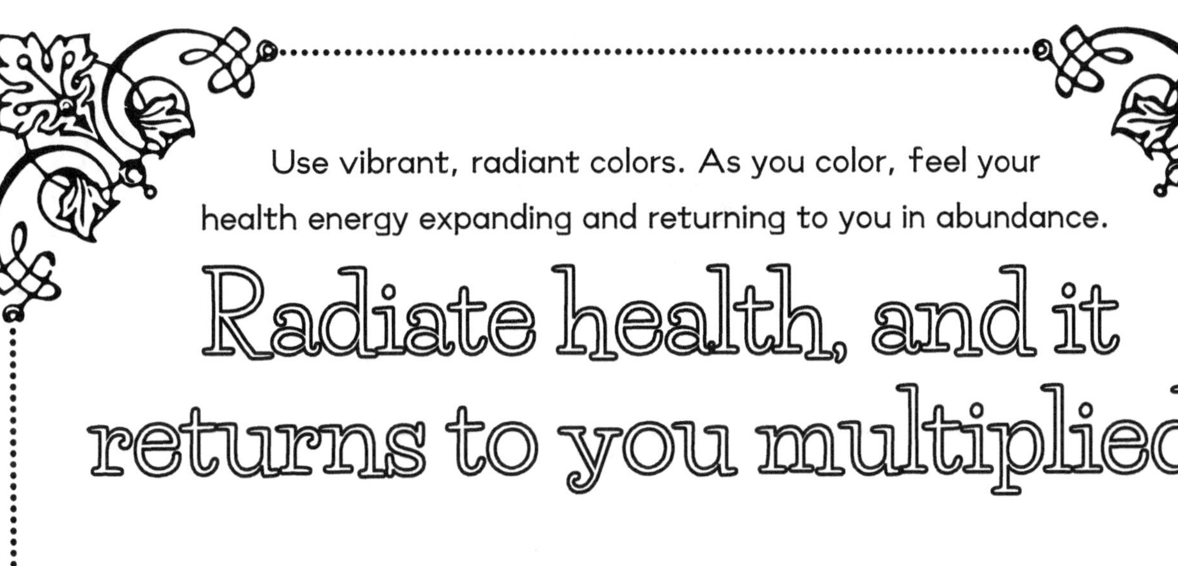

Use vibrant, radiant colors. As you color, feel your health energy expanding and returning to you in abundance.

Radiate health, and it returns to you multiplied!

I am grateful for:

My manifestation:

VISION BOARD

As you color, imagine surrounding yourself
with self-love and kindness.
You are deserving your
own love and kindness!

I am grateful for:

My manifestation:

VISION BOARD

As you color, envision yourself attracting
self-acceptance and self-compassion.
Effortlessly attract
self-improvement!

I am grateful for:

My manifestation:

VISION BOARD

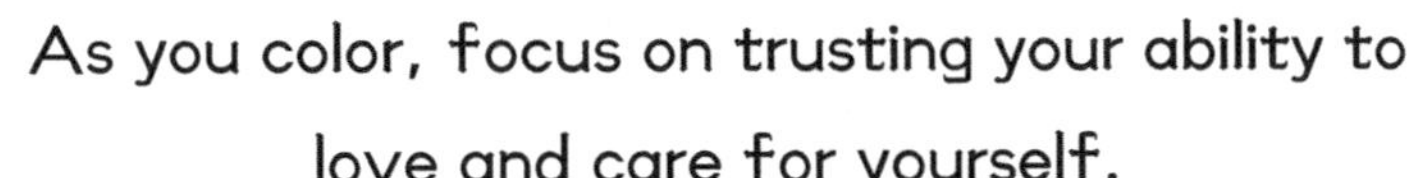

As you color, focus on trusting your ability to
love and care for yourself.

Trust your ability to love and care for yourself!

I am grateful for:

My manifestation:

VISION BOARD

As you color, repeat affirmations of unconditional
self-love and self-acceptance.

You are complete, love
yourself unconditionally!

I am grateful for:

My manifestation:

VISION BOARD

As you color, feel yourself worthy of
financial success and money.
You are deserving
financial success!

I am grateful for:

My manifestation:

VISION BOARD

As you color, imagine your life as the greatest financial story ever written, with self-love and abundance as the central theme.

You are your own greatest life story!

I am grateful for:

My manifestation:

VISION BOARD

As you color, affirm that wellness is your birthright,
and you claim it with love.

Wellness is your birthright,
claim it with love!

"The seeds of your
actions bloom into the
garden of your destiny."